Reflections

Poetry & Prose
about Everyday life
2.0

SG Williams
BSc.(Hons) RAc.

ABOUT

This is a collection of poems spanning five decades based on the everyday life experiences of the author. From child rearing and poems for her young children, to observations of human nature and beyond. Both the silly and the serious topics are covered from the depth of pain to the heights of joy. There is something here for everyone.

DEDICATION

This was published for my three children Robb, Jill and Tracy who are now grown up with lives and children of their own.

CONTENTS

1 LITTLE ONES

Stinky Feet

Pink little piggies.
Those ten tiny toes.
Beautiful little feet,
All bare and cold.

Mommy will hold them,
To warm them up.
Oh my goodness!
Oh poo wee!

How could this happen?
These tiny feet stink.
It's time for a bath,
A little wash in the sink.

Wash Up

Wash a face,

Scrub a face,

Rub, rub, rub.

In the ears,

Behind the ears,

Around we go.

Don't forget your sleepy eyes.

Don't forget your mouth.

Scrub our little cheeks,

Our forehead, chin and nose.

Breakfast

Hungry little children,
Want something to eat.
Their tummies are rumbling,
But they want candies and treats.

Sorry, no sweets!
Off that shelf, don't fall!
Eating treats for breakfast,
Will make you stay small!

For breakfast we need grow food,
To make you tall.
It is cereal and milk.
Toast with peanut butter and jam.

And the most favourite, eggs!
Hold in hand eggs, Peek-a-boo eggs
And eggs all messed up.
Always tasty eaten out of a cup.

Get Dressed

I wonder, wonder where?

I wonder where the underwear went?

Yes, I wonder where the underwear went?

Over by the bed?

Behind the door?

I know they were here,

Just a moment ago.

Jillian's Hair

Oh! tangle angle Oh!

A tangle in Jillian's hair.

There is a tangle in little Jillian's hair.

A tangle in her beautiful blonde hair.

We brush it and

We brush it.

We put a tail in it,

With a pretty purple thingy,

We make some curly whorls,

In Jillian's ponytail.

Call to Bed

Bedtime for Robbie!

Bedtime for Jillian!

Bedtime for Tracy too!

Everyone is sleepy.

Not more TV.

No more little stories for you.

Time to turn the lights out.

Time to go to sleep now.

Tomorrow we have lots to do.

Monsters

Dear little Robbie,
Don't you dread.
There are no monsters,
Under your bed.

They are only in stories,
Or in your mind.
Please don't be worried,
There are none I can find.

Keep your eyes tightly shut.
Just cover your head.
They will think you are gone,
If they look at your bed.

In any case...,
Don't worry, just sleep.
The monsters Mommy knows,
Are gentle and sweet.

The Quiet Child

Quiet and gentle,
Is what we say,
About that child who,
Loves to run and play.

Her arms flailing high and low
Her voice screaming,
"You so and so...!"
One minute smile, the next pouting.

The sparkle in her eyes,
Reveal a wild imagination.
As she draws or builds,
Her newest creation.

She cocks her head,
With big innocent eyes,
"What is that you said...?"
"I can't hear you ....", she tries.

Laughter follows her presence.
Quiet she isn't you see.
Her love is quite evident,
She is God's gift to me.

Kyle

A wish, a hope, a dream.

Life's touch, a small hand.

Laid down lightly, gently.

For a moment of time,

A Spirit's desire glowed brightly,

Then extinguished,

Like a shooting star.

Rocking My Babies

Rock a baby Jillian.
Rock a baby Robbie.
Rock a baby Tracy three.
Mommy loves her little girls.
Mommy loves her big boy.

Rock my babies,
Go to sleep.
I love to hold you.
My babies, three.

Please don't wiggle,
Or try to get down.
Soon you'll be all grown up,
With lives of your own.

Eternal Youth

The Secret:
Remember how you saw the world
as a child.

Re-live the wonder.

Re-see the beauty.

Re-set your heart to
Re-feel the joy.

2 PEOPLE

The Bus

The bus arrives, Metro Transit,
Elbows vie for position, advantage.
A seat I must have,
For the Halifax voyage.

The mob pushes towards the door.
Should men give way first?
But the weather's too cold.
Each man for himself.
There is little room for more.

Some don't mind,
A place by the pole
Being forced rearward and rearward.,
With each new step onboard.

A chatter between friends, above roar.
"I'd tell him where to go...!"
A headphone overflowing,
Tiny sounds of rock and roll.
And traffic as always is slow.

A ding!, a squeal, a hiss of the door.
Musical chairs, then a scramble,
Bus lurches forward, footing unsure.
Forty minutes before seats become ample.

Although potential for conversation,
Most hide behind silent masks.
Minding your own is the first consideration.
Sharing is not offered and nobody asks.

Faces stare blankly,
At windows and books
Glances indifferent.,
Guarded by aloofness and looks.

But as soon as each one,
Reaches their world, their own stop,
They awake from their slumber,
Quickly fleeing with a skip and hop.

Old Man

It is strange,
The way he sits.
He sits staring, gazing.
It seems, at nothing.

But he sees many things.
For he is a man
Old and wise.

He sits and listens,
And hears.

This age of prosperity,
Are deaf and blind.

They do not hear ,
What the old man hears.

Ears are deafened,
By the jingle of money,
The ticking of time.

The old man hears,
The cries of the sick,
And the voices of the lonely.

The others only see,
What they want to see.

They only hear,
What they want to hear.

Nobody has time,
To listen and understand.

Bride & Groom

Oh what glorious wonder,

When two heart's become knit forever.

As if always meant to be.

Predestined as the skies and sea.

Such a mystery,

Is just a clue.

Of the gift of love,

For the both of you.

Flicker in Time

We laugh, we plan, we play,
Working diligently.
Building, establishing,
Busying ourselves,
With abandonment.

Carefree, carousing,
Tasting this, testing that.
Feeling, experiencing,
Whatever we choose,
And what we choose not.

Talking, listening,
Thinking, reminiscing.
Slowing down,
To consider and wonder.
Searching for the best.

So much joy.
So much heartache.
Emptiness, regrets.
So much to do.
So little time.

My Beloved

Who knew?
God answered true.
When my angel appeared,
Dressed in a ball cap and blue.

His voice booming,
Against bad politics.
Dreaming of pistons,
Rpm and engine tics.

With wheels,
Of rubber turning.
And the sword of truth,
Blazing and burning!

This man of integrity and honour.
My beloved and my own,
With whom I forever belong.
Who makes this house a home.

3 NATURE

Wind

Gently the wind blows,

As it whispers to the trees,

Beautiful secrets.

Fog

Greying and misty,

Is the fog in the early morning,

Dulling the new sunlight.

Ocean

Giant pounding waves,

Crash viciously against the cliffs,

And quickly retreat.

Fall Leaves

Colours bright,

An explosion of hue,

Yellow, red and orange.

Singing a song of vibrancy.

A celebration of beauty.

A sign that all was well done.

Nature's last triumphant symphony,

Inflames the forests,

As hints of snow hang in the air.

The Mayflower

Delicate clusters,
With tiny petals blushing,
Lie huddled and prostate,
beneath layered curled awning.

Defiant and hardy,
Buffered from severity,
With a sweet wondrous aroma,
From heaven's tiny windows.

Heralds of spring..
Nature's miniature messengers
Welcome the beauty of new birth,
In both splendour and humility.

Night Storm

It was deathly still and quiet.
Dark clouds brewed on the horizon.

The brisk wind gently died
And there was silence.
Except for the murmuring of the trees.

Ghostly shadows danced along the,
Ground, as the sky beckoned.

The clouds slipped around the moon,
And darkness flooded the earth.

Rain gently started tapping my face.
Then like tiny drums, it woke,
The sleeping surface of the lake.

Then the charcoal horizon,
Was shattered with a violent light,
Cracking open the silence of the night.

Thunder rumbled the earth,
And trembled in the cool moist air.

Then the cloak of darkness and silence,
Fell over the earth again.

Day of the Hyena

The old hyena lay smothered in blood.
Motionless except for one brown eye.
Watching the vultures falling, swooping,
Down from the morning sky.

Around her lay plains of drought.
The air is increasingly hot and dry.
Where the waking trees lay silhouetted,
As the sun escaped from beneath the sky.

The old hyena watched, covered in scars,
Ears drooped, ripped and soar.
The right eye stared sightless into space,
Head aching from battle two days before.

In desperate search of food for her cubs,
She wandered forty miles of rugged terrain.
She was once a proud leader in her pack,
Until others sensed her growing age and pain.

Alert in her half-sleep, midday came and left.
A steady plodding revealed a young lion.
She awaited the chance and followed him.
She continued for hours until the shrill crying.

When the lion leapt, the baboon died.
But impatience grew,she couldn't stay placed.
She bared her teeth and darted forward.
She grabbed the meat and attempted to escape.

She was too slow for the big cat.
He uttered a snarl as the giant paw fell.
Narrowly missing, as she wheeled away.
Her life depends on her success, expelled.

Her actions brought other hyenas closer.
Soon the grass was licked clean.
Then dawn touches the sky a coral pink.
She returned home, broken and lean.

The old hyena lay smothered in mud.
Motionless except for one brown eye.
Watching the vultures falling, swooping,
Invisible to the world, as life passed her by.

The Earth

The cycle of the earth breathes,
The energy of birth, growth and decline.

We too undergo a cycle of transformation,
That is beautiful and perfect.

Awaken to this rebirth.
Become aware of your magnificence.

Love yourself wholly.
Accept the spirit of the universe,
That is at the core of who you are.

Be in awe of every moment.

See the magic in the ordinary.

Cherish what you behold with new eyes.

Feel the peace of gratitude envelop you.

Listen to your heart.

Seek your true self,
By dissolving the fog of the world.

Know that you are perfect just as you are,
Wonderfully made and specially purposed.

Love the Earth.

Embrace joy even in the most difficult times.

Know that you are loved,
Even if it is not love from this world.

Laugh, sing, dance and heal.

Watch as your passions,
Fulfill your deepest desires and
Know that you can create,
The world of your dreams.

4 SPIRIT & LOVE

Five Tenets

1.0 - What is wisdom but self knowledge and introspection into the soul's connection to love?

2.0 - What is love but empathy and compassion for self and others through faith, hope and justice?

3.0 - What is justice but compassionate correction and healing through fairness, kindness, charity, forgiveness and truth?

4.0 - What causes suffering but hate, injustice and despair?

5.0 - What conquers all suffering but love through wisdom?

.

Knowledge2

The futility of knowledge.

It strengthens the mind,

And confuses the heart,

It is a stumbling block.

To the doorway to the soul.

Self Love

Be kind to yourself.

Forgive your own imperfections.

You are uniquely made.

You have a special destiny.

Reflect on the good in you.

Accept the many facets of love.

It is time to receive and be
grateful for the gifts the universe
has made for you.

Spirit

Spirit circles around us,to protect the vulnerable.

Inspiring good deeds and hope to the lost children.

Raging against a cruel world.

The Spirit hovers, protecting, guarding even when the benefactor does not believe.

As they look for love.

Hoping someone will notice them.

Spirit pours out its kindness.

Caring for the forgotten.

Never giving up.

Never abandoning such treasured souls.

Grace

An invisible force that cannot be explained.
The mind cannot comprehend it.
No amount of study,
No detailed pictures,
No articulate descriptions,
Will suffice.

Yet it is a colourless ether that can be known.
The heart can feel it enter therein.
It is a weighty presence of unlimited size.
A gentle warming from places unknown.
It is the sensation of AWE magnified.

It can never be acquired.
Yet it is freely given.
Bestowed upon those who ask for it.

For those who ask,
The manifestation may be a large event,
Or as tiny as a whisper.

It is always a surprise.
That takes time to recognize
And humility to behold.

Its power is remarkable.
Witnesses claim it changes heart,
Alters motives.

Transforming the receiver.
Allows their best self to shine forth.

Bringing goodness in its wake.

It cannot be manufactured.
Nore scientifically tested.
But it is real.

It is like the reflection in a mirror.
Or the glow of love.

It draws people to itself,
As it emanates from those who possess it.

This priceless commodity,
Is not for the rich and powerful.
But for the faithful that accept His grace.

Heart's Discovery

Who's voice is this?
That argues with self.
The advocate?
The agitator?
Or somebody else?

The Mind takes in
All it can see.
It analyzes, it knows,
Creates stories
And personalities.

It has a reason to be.

However conflict arises
Between action
And intention.
Motive versus rationale
Creates discord and tension.

The Ego declares
"I am most important, you see!"
Conscience says "not true"
While Emotions are worried
About others in need.

Who are these players?
Am I crazy or deceived?
As the Heart answers truly:
"You are a Triumvirate, in harmony
With the power of three".

The facilitator of these entities,
The one who sees this thus.
Not the Mind, Ego or Conscience.
Not even the Emotions.
This is the voice of the Us.

This is the You voice.
Behind the Mind and the Ego.
The true self that sees the players.
The real you as a witness
In the omnipresent ether.

5 SELF KNOWLEDGE

Choices

Pilots of souls choosing death's road,
Are directed by the living dead,
To travel familiar darkened caverns,
Where stagnating reality,
Painfully echoes,
Against narrow empty walls.

Pilots of souls choosing life's path,,
Are called by the wind,
To soar beyond earthly limits,
Where the fulfillment of dreams,
Joyfully extends,
To the glory of Heaven.

Heart

The pulse of life,
Propels us forward,
Through maze and twisted bend.
Attuned to strife,
Planned collaborations are horrid.

The heart is unable to mend.
Disabled by fear,
Grasping for answers.
When that ray of light,
A calm moment does send.

Illumination and failure is thwarted.
Disaster averted.
Strength to the end.
Our power lies not in our trust of men,
But in the Truth that carries us homeward.

Purpose

It is our purpose and destiny
to live in conscious oneness with
our world, be present and know that
our true identity is in the reflection
of the divine.

When your non-persona can tap into
your passion and your actions are
directed by love, inspiration and
enthusiasm, your work will resonate
in alignment with the goals of the universe.

This is the secret to knowing your life
purpose, that you can fulfill every day that
you have the courage to be true to what
you know what is right.

Once realized, it will change everything.
In this way you will change the world
with more power than you ever imagined.

Awaken

Discover the spirit within.
Awaken to that battle of
Thinking versus knowing.

Resist the hate of the world.

Plant your roots deep.
Reach to the mountains and
Remember who you are.

Stoke the fires of truth.

Don the bow of righteousness.
Take up your quiver full,
Of faith, hope and justice.

Hear the cries for true peace.

Hoist your lantern.
Expose the evil and requite,
Heart's longings to do what is right.

In the Zone

The better you get at being you,
The more you can help others find themselves.

This synergy of goodness can grow
Like a tsunami of love paid forward.

Watch your authentic self at work.

Know that when you follow your passion,
You are in the zone.

Like a surfer riding a wave
That will help heal the world.

The Power

Our power comes from knowing
and understanding ourselves.

Accepting what we learn.

Then having courage and strength,
to direct our actions,
in alignment
with who we are.

6 PAIN

The Struggle

Though a young, twenty-something,
My heart aches,
From the wounds inflicted by my enemies,
Whose numbers are great.
I am surrounded day and night.
Sometimes my heart feels faint.
I have no place to hide,
From the rage of hate against me.

I do not know what I have done.
Or why I am hated so.
Most people I encounter try to harm me.
I am slandered, ridiculed and scorned.
I am a victim of thieves,
Who circle me like vultures.

Am I mad to think that evil forces,
Plan my destruction?
I imagine various conspiracies.
Then upon investigation,
I find them to be true,
Only more horrible than imagined.
If I speak of these things,
Know one would believe me.

I trust know one except,
The Lord my God.
He is my only hope and salvation.
To Him do I cling.
As wretched as I am,
He has showered me with,

His great mercy and love.
Blessed be my God .
Who will not let my,
Enemies consume me.

Bullying

It occurs in many places and situations.

It is often not recognized as bullying

It hides behind supposed "acts of kindness" or "just joking".

It pretends to be helpful or concerned.

It uses "good" deeds to cover evil intentions.

It is a terrible menacing action.

It is an impassioned, collective campaign.

It is the act of cowards who exclude, punish, and humiliate their target.

It travels through the workplace or community like a virus, infecting others.

Until the victim is viewed as a terrible monster, with no redeeming qualities.

Madness

Driven by a voice buried in the
Mystery of my soul.

I am compelled to reach and
Touch broken lives.

Like a song bursting from my breast
I want to say "I love you!"

I want to shout to the world ,
"If only if it would love, there
Would be hope".

If I could release my intentions,
I would give everything to
Those in need.

I want to draw close to the unlovely,
To believe in everyone, to listen,
Hear heart's longings and
Fulfill them.

I want to give hope by deed or
Spoken word.

The life within me says to give it all
For that is the substance of joy.

Is love strongest when it is poured
Rather than left to steep?

What is the cost to truly live and
Truly love?

I must pay all, but can I?

What are the consequences of such
Madness in a world like this?

Instead, I survive sensibly.
I behave reasonably and realistically.

I am too rational for such a sacrifice.

Fear restrains me.

Selfishness binds me.

Twisted conformity artificially
Moulds me and I allow it.

However living without this madness
Is horror and living with it is pain.

I am torn between dying to myself
So that I might truly live or focusing
On myself so the true joy will die.

This is the madness love calls me to.

Pandemic

The void is expansive, dark and heavy.

Resonating in hearts of the
Collective grief.

As a counter-life avalanche,
Marches, consumes and extinguishes.

Tiny soldiers permeate the earth,
Blocking light with a cloak of retribution,
Entitled masses in selfish gaiety,
Deny the silencing of the vulnerable.

Time screams loud and long.

Calling for retracing the steps of our
existence.

Re- evaluate the wanton disrespect for
the delicate balance of our Great Mother.

Take us back to the garden.

Let us reconsider lusting for knowledge,
Over the omnipotent benevolence
That fills, illuminates and completes us.

The Path

Know you are on the right path even if having never committed an offence, you are hunted down, constructively punished with no regard for the facts.

Seeking the truth is never popular among those who hide behind masks. Especially self-servers who congregate, vowing to silence you at any costs, using taxpayer funds and even abuses of power and allies in positions of trust.

Such a clamouring of haters is the harbinger that your way is true.

Know you are an eternal lighthearted soul, laughing and skipping stones on the surface of the pond, with no fear of the unhappy sludge dwellers below.

Your soul can never be harmed and attempts to endanger or destroy self-worth, only deepens your joy as spirit draws closer.

Continue quietly therefore, grounded in the steadfast source with an eye for potholes created by lost souls.

The greatest opposition comes in the presence of the biggest miracles.

Peaceful Wishes

In these difficult days:

Love calls us
To rise above the fear
And see that we are
Much more powerful
Than on the surface
Does appear.

So on this frosty holiday eve,
I think of you and yours.
Wishing you the peace,
The blessings
And the courage
The loving heart
Truly knows.

Wounds That Bind

Every wound,

Is another dab of mortar.

Binding us together

With the rest of humanity.

The world within us,

Will teach us everything,

About the world without.

Loss & Found

It was in the loss of self,
that a connection to divinity was discovered.

It was in the deepest darkness,
That a glorious light was revealed.

It was in the middle of
the most difficult trials and suffering,
that was found
The most intense peace
And profound joy.

7 INJUSTICE

Invisible

I work hard, I am diligent,
I enjoy what I do.
My ideas are good ones.
The results are efficient..

When know one asks,
I volunteer.
I've met with successes,
Year after year.

But achievements are forgotten,
Again and again.
I must always step forward,
With each mew begin.

I remind coworkers,
I really am able.
Even though with my training,
Such tasks should be natural.

But as hard as I try,
To be a cog in the wheel,
I am placed on some shelf,
A spare part, piecemeal.

Am I mindless, invisible,
Or just too quiet.
When listener turns mid-sentence,
To a new face, new topic.

There must be rewards,

But promotions pass by me.
Make the coffee they say.
Valued tasks I rarely see.

What is wrong with me,
That things must be so.
I'm called aggressive, ambitious,
And what else, who knows?

They say I threaten, intimidate,
And so I must tip toe,
Around various egos,
As fragile as snow.

But unfortunately my real self,
Slips from the mould,
And escapes in enthusiasm,
To act on some goal.

The result is chagrin,
All progress is ended,
When another poor soul,
Has been duly offended.

At just over five feet,
Regardless of stature,
A monster I am ,
To inflict such disaster.

My intentions are good,
Honest and true.
I desire to do duty,
And let peace be the rule.

But I've come know,

These problems aren't mine.
What can I do?
If I'm not the right kind.

I must learn to be patient,
Some minds just won't bend.
It is not easy being a woman,
In a world ruled by men.

Beautiful Morning

Thus beautiful morning
The kids play and play...
Get dressed I say.
The taxi won't wait!

A squirming foot,
And one left shoe,
Books, Betty doll and four toy cars.
We shuffle out the door.

Hurry up, hurry up!
In go bodies, books, doll, toy cars,
Cabbie backs out,
While we search for seat belts.

Oh no!, the wrong way.
Do I say anything?
No, what the heck.
I can afford the extra fifty cents.

The kids sit, quietly,
Restrained in their seats.
We adults chit, chat.
Old familiar small talk

"What a beautiful morning",
I say to Cabbie.
"Yes, autumn is glorious
My favourite time of year."

Then the tone changes,

As the driver tells me a tale.
Yes, he was really pissed off,
At a past fare.

Insolent the fare was,
To ask if he knew the way.
He neared throwing her out,
 Leaving her in the lurch.

"She was a white woman", he said.
But he knew she was living,
With a black man.
A "The N word", he announced.

I felt a jolt, at the words.
I was catapulted,
Back in time,
To the days of slavery.

He said he had little respect
For a white girl
Who would give herself,
To "The N word", he repeated.

I saw his eyes in his rear view mirror,
Looking to me,
For that mutual understanding.
Being white, he assumed I agreed.

I glanced quickly away,
Could he see the horror,
In my blank stare.
My heart beat quickly.

What should I do?

What should I say?
He must be wondering,
Why do I remain so silent?

Do I tell him,
I am offended, shocked?
I feel as though,
I was that woman, that past fare.

Monetarily, my husband,
Is that black man.
I'm embarrassed, shaken.
I want to defend him.

How dare you call,
Him a "The N word"!
We are really all the same,
This you must know!

But I say nothing.
He wouldn't listen anyway.
He would probably get angry.
Who am I to judge?, I justify.

Yes, it was a beautiful day.
But now I can't breathe,
In my silence,
I am an accessory to the crime.

He doesn't see ,
The grotesque nature,
The death, the hate,
Such attitudes breed.

The sun is still shining,

As it did ten minutes ago.
The kids are quiet, half listening,
Watching pets, people and cars.

Arriving, kids scramble to get out.
Books, Betty and four toy cars.
My mind is scrambling, questioning,
Is it fear that makes people act so?

Conquering Fear

I can't believe it!
Here I am again,
In the cross hairs,
Of another evil plot.
Like deja vu.

This time will be different.
I am ready.
I have moved past the,
Signs flashing danger,
Telling me to be afraid.

This time fear,
Will not stop me in my tracks.
It will not hold me back,
From slipping up,
And into my real power.

After all, the consequences,
Are not that bad.
Public humiliation,
Piled on by slanders and haters,
Like walking naked in public.

The worst has been done.
It is the cowardly bullies and perjurers,

Who should be afraid?
Karma can be really nasty.
Someday, they will have to answer.
Not me.

I have answered to my higher power.
I know who I am.
I am forgiven.
I am innocent,
Acquitted of the false accusations.

It is time to let go,
Of those last remnants of concern,
Of the opinions of others.
Time to wield my power,
Stand firm and hold strong.

My small, quiet, feminine form,
Belies the raging courage within.
A patriarchal Druid in disguise,
Ready to fight, ready to right,
The wrongs of our time.

OMG

OMG in the past I was able,
To open a file, a life story, a fable,
Share spirit and advise as was able,
Then leave travesty on the table.

OMG now I am confined to four walls,
Sent here by bullies and liars.
Present to the haunting voices in halls.
Many in crisis, I can't ignore the calls.

OMG why are some women here?
Victims of circumstance, abuse and fear.
Hidden from society, pushed to the rear.
Away from imagined justice-by-peers.

OMG my heart aches for innocence taken.
Just children who love failed to beckon.
Judges "just-us" is punishment meted.
Anger from unfairness is to be expected.

OMG news, past wrongs coming to light.
Many damages, no apologies, no fight.
This culture of inequity, a massive blight.
It needs love and courage to make it right.

Warrior

Confidence unfailing.
She radiates strength.

Powered by the depths of,
Self-knowledge,
Her mind is trained,
To challenge, question.

Instinctively she tests,
The feelings surrounding her.
Her heart is attentive,
To the needs of others.

Experience has taught.
There is a time to stand,
And a time to back down.

Alien systems, expectations,
Often demand and dictate,
A woman's sacrifice.

Wisdom teaches her that giving is joy.
But to give everything is void and death.

Some are threatened by her demeanour.
She defies their assumptions,
of a rightful place.

She exposes their humanness.
Superior masks are challenged, removed.
False egos waver and falter,

In her presence.

Those filled with fear and self doubt,
Arm themselves with aggression.
They assert their demands.

Those so affected ask concessions.
They demand weakness in return.
After all history has dictated,
Such cooperation.

She is expected to sooth ,
Appease her aggressors.
Her arrogant attitude,
Improper, inappropriate.
We can't have such a rebellion here.

Obedience demands great loss.
Should she throw hands up in despair,
Or do battle?
Instant peace is easy.
But peace for whom?

The childish games are over.
True peace will only come
When all things are reconciled.
Even if through fire.

Destiny

When she knows her true identity,
Is in the reflection of the divine.

When her spirit binds with passion,
Love and the courage to do what is right.

Only then will she wield ,
That sword of power to change destiny.

The tsunami her soul creates,
Will disrupt corrupt institutions.

Her piercing light will expose,
Those that protect the takers.

Her integrity will throw shame,
On the liars and the haters.

Then the wake of revolution ,
Will ignite others who have had enough.

8 JOY & TRIUMPH

New Day

Every day can be a new day,

If we are present to receive it.

The past is just a thread,

That ties us to our learning,

To gird us in the journey forward.

Not bind us.

The Gift

The present day is all we have.

The past is gone.

The future holds no promises.

Today is the gift of a new beginning.

So behold the wonder of life.

Be grateful for small blessings.

Expect wonderful possibilities.

The Stars

The angels whose glorious light abounds,
Reveal to me, a sweet mystery profound.
Those who hail the wondrous Trinity,
And sing to Its triumphant Majesty,
Reserve great reverence and praise,
Not for the heavenly beings so raised,
But for the mortal souls that suffer much.

Choosing to believe,
Faith wavering to trust.
Despite great evil,
To virtue they cling.
Amidst humanities din,
They hear love sing.
Surrounded by hate,
They do the best they can.
Faintly still loving their fellow man.

It is these that the angels tell,
Who are the ones that will defeat,
The gates of hell.
Struggling against all odds to be ready,
With hearts strong and spirits steady,
Is is these the angels say,
That are the chosen stars that,
Will light our way.

Stay Strong

Be courageous to stand apart,
From the crowd.
Resist the pull of the anger of the mob.

Gravitate to the light that illuminates,
The world.

Trim your wick and keep your,
Lanterns bright.

Always be ready to defend the truth.

Cultivate a deep love for yourself.
Hold fast to what you know is good.

Know there is beauty and hope.
Seek unconditional love to combat hate.

Feel empathy for those who have,
Lost their way.

Be generous with kindness to,
Those in need.

Have faith that justice will prevail.

Rise Up x3

Educate yourself
so you can act Intelligently.

Find Courage so you can take action.

Work at Forgiveness to untangle the past
for clarity of forward vision.

Learn Empathy and compassion
to wield love more effectively.

Practice Gratitude to fuel
Faith and perseverance.

Cherish all these
to Rise Up with the power of three.

Be True

Be true to yourself.

Follow the joy.

Believe your intuition.

Feel the fear.

And do it anyway.

Heed The Call

Madness swirls around us,
Like dark clouds,
Obscuring the light and,
Confusing the truth,
With judgment and hate.

Listen, heed the signs,
And escape the madness.
Know that you are the light,
That will not be snuffed out,
By the evil of these strange times.

Return to love.
Climb to the higher ground,
Of righteousness.
Save yourself, your soul and,
Answer love's call.

Triumphant Affirmation

I am respected.

I am loved.

I am validated.

I am vindicated.

I am exonerated.

I am healthy.

I am healed.

I am free.

I am one with the universe and,

The universe is in me.

Happiness Is

Accepting yourself as you are.

Realizing each day is a gift.

Reflecting on abundant blessings.

Feeling proud of accomplishments.

Enjoying the natural beautiful surroundings.

Having courage to create positive change.

Using your skills to help and support others.

Knowing you are loved no matter what.

Transformation

Life is a series of cycles
of transformation and perfection.

Accept the rebirth.

Be in awe of each moment.

Let peace and gratitude envelop you.

See the beauty of your true self
in the still waters of your soul.

Know that you are perfect just as you are,
wonderfully made and uniquely loved.

ABOUT THE AUTHOR

SG Williams has spent decades working in science, research, technology and continuously studying as a life-long learner. It has only been in the last decade she has worked in the public eye as a quasi part-time activist trying to bring peace and wellness to the community.

She believes in simplicity, authenticity, inner peace and keeping the wonder of life alive by paying attention to our surroundings. She sees every person as unique and specially created with something important to teach us. In her opinion it is imperative for everyone to have access to healthy communities, where people can be appreciated for who they are, free from injustice and discrimination.

Now, through her books, she hopes to offer emotional validation for those who are suffering. She hopes that she can be a voice for change or a catalyst for others to speak out, by describing the injustices she sees, experiences and hears through the stories of others.